WRITING BASICS

Sentence to Paragraph to Essay

Sandra Panman, M.P.S.
State University of New York at New Paltz

Richard Panman, Ph.D.
State University of New York at New Paltz

Active Learning Corporation
New Paltz, New York
(914) 255-0844

Writing Basics
Sentence to Paragraph to Essay

Copyright © 1996, 1991, 1988 by Sandra Panman and Richard Panman

All rights reserved in all countries. No part of this publication may be translated, reproduced, or transmitted in any form or by any means, electronic or mechanical, including photocopy, recording, or any information storage and retrieval system, without permission in writing from the publisher.

Address all inquiries to:
Active Learning Corporation
P.O. Box 254
New Paltz, New York 12561
(914) 255-0844

Text Design and Editing: Linda Gluck
Art Director: Elena Erber
Illustrators: Kirk Van Deusen, Camy Fischer

Printed in the United States of America/vg95
ISBN: 0-912813-24-5

Acknowledgments

For permission to reprint copyrighted material, grateful acknowledgment is made to the following sources:

Atlantic Monthly Company: Excerpted from "The Scarlet Ibis" by James Hurst. Copyright © 1960, by the Atlantic Monthly Company, Boston, Mass. Reprinted with permission.

A. S. Barnes & Company, Inc. and Kaye & Ward Ltd.: From *Modern Spearfishing* by I.S. Ivanovic. Copyright © 1955 by A. S. Barnes & Company, Inc.

Ray Bradbury: Excerpted from "A Sound of Thunder." Copyright © 1952 by Ray Bradbury Enterprises/A California Corporation.

Faber & Faber, Ltd.: Excerpted from *As I Saw the U.S.A.* by Jan Morris. Copyright © 1956.

Random House, Inc.: Excerpted from *Sentence Combining: A Composing Book* by William Strong. Copyright © 1973 by Random House, Inc.

William Saroyan: Excerpted from "An Ornery Kind of Kid" by William Saroyan. Reprinted with permission by the estate of William Saroyan.

Contents

How To Use This Book 4

To The Teacher 5

The Complete Sentence 9

Answering Questions 18

Transitional Words and Phrases 23

Combining Sentences 30

Expanding Sentences 40

Paragraph Development 50

The Narrative Paragraph 55

The Descriptive Paragraph 60

The Expository Paragraph 66

Using Examples 72

Using Definition 77

Comparison and Contrast 82

Cause and Effect 89

The Persuasive Paragraph 95

The Essay 101

List of Transitions 109

Answer Key 113

How To Use This Book

The goal of **Writing Basics** is to help you learn to write well-crafted sentences, paragraphs, and essays. The first guided lesson teaches how to write complete sentences. The next guide provides instruction on how to answer questions in complete sentences. This is followed by a lesson about transitional words and phrases which shows how to connect ideas in writing. The use of transitions is essential if you want to write paragraphs that make sense and are well written.

Combining sentences is a technique that teaches you how to connect short, simple sentences in order to make more interesting ones. Each activity gives you something to write about and challenges you to write it in the best way possible. As with transitional words and phrases, you can use sentence combining to link ideas and create unity in your writing. Expanding sentences, like combining sentences, helps you to add meaning to a simple sentence. When we expand a sentence, we make it more meaningful by offering detailed information about who, what, where, when, and why.

Once you have completed the lessons on writing sentences, you are prepared to write paragraphs. All paragraphs have a beginning, middle, and end. How you write the paragraph, the strategy you use, depends on your purpose. If you want to tell a story, use narration. If you want to create vivid images for the reader, use description. If you want to explain facts or ideas, use exposition. If you want to convince the reader to see things your way, use persuasion. These are four major writing strategies you will learn to use.

Guides to other writing strategies in this book include: Using Examples, Using Definition, Comparison and Contrast, and Cause and Effect. These strategies follow the lesson on exposition because they are often used to explain facts or ideas. They can also be used in writing narration, description, and persuasion. For example, you could tell a story using comparison and contrast, or you could try to convince someone of something by showing how causes lead to effects. The last lesson in the book, The Essay, shows you how to apply what you know about writing paragraphs to writing essays.

Each guide in the book begins with a model of the type of writing you will learn to master. Read the model and complete the Practice exercises that follow. Score the exercise using the answer key. These prewriting activities prepare you for the composition assignment. Follow the plan or outline provided in each lesson to write your first draft. Use the Checklist as a way of evaluating and revising your own work before you submit it to the teacher for review.

If you are using the book on your own, outside of a classroom setting, no teacher will be available to evaluate your work. Ask a person whose opinion you respect—a friend, colleague, or relative—to read your papers and give you feedback. Ask them to tell you what they learned from your paper, what they liked and disliked about it, and what was clear or unclear about the paper. Make revisions based on their comments and the Checklist in each lesson.

To The Teacher

"How To Use This Book" provides an overview of the text for both student and teacher. In addition, several points relevant mainly to the instructor are grouped together here. These concern guidelines for instructor feedback and suggestions for brainstorming and peer critiquing. We suggest that students keep all writing in a looseleaf binder or a writing folder. Upon completion of this text, students will have compiled a visible record of their work and progress in your class.

Feedback from the teacher can have a very powerful and positive effect in motivating the student to learn. Make sure students understand your system for evaluating and grading papers. To gain students' trust and confidence, try to give them the good news first, followed by your constructive criticisms. The good news is praise for at least one aspect of the student's paper: ideas, choice of subject, enthusiasm, neat handwriting, etc.

When there are many errors in a paper, focus on three or four of the most frequent ones. As these are eliminated, you can point out others. Try not to overwhelm your students with criticism before they develop confidence in their ability to write. Written comments should be specific enough for the student to make changes and corrections in their work. You may also want to speak with the student in a brief, one-to-one informal conference in class. Conferences allow for discussion and direct exchange of ideas.

Two valuable and enjoyable classroom activities that you can use with the text are brainstorming and peer critiquing. While composition exercises provide suggested topics, you may wish to have students "brainstorm" as a group to generate other topics. From time to time, complete compositions can be critiqued by the peer group. Prepare students for this by sharing the feedback guidelines above and encouraging constructive criticism. Peer critiquing gives students an opportunity to sharpen their listening and speaking skills, as well as improve writing ability.

WRITING BASICS

Sentence to Paragraph to Essay

The Complete Sentence

This guide will help you to recognize and write complete sentences. A sentence expresses a complete thought. In writing a sentence, you might make a statement, ask a question, tell someone to do something, or express strong feeling.

Practice

Read each part of the following exercises and answer all **30** questions. This lesson begins with a look at three kinds of sentences: simple, compound, and complex.

The Simple Sentence

A **simple** sentence has a subject and a verb. The subject is *who* or *what* the sentence is about. The verb tells us what the subject *does, its condition,* or *where it is*. Identify the subject and verb in the simple sentences below. The first one is done for you.

The cook flipped the pancakes.
subject: cook
verb: flipped

The log floats down the river.
1. subject: verb:

The food is hot.
2. subject: verb:

The marbles spilled onto the floor.
3. subject: verb:

In the sentences above, you identified a simple subject and a simple predicate (the verb). The simple subject and information about it is called the **subject**. The simple predicate and information about it is called the **predicate**, or **verb**. The subject and predicate are identified in the example below.

                  Subject **Predicate**

           (who or what) (what is said about the subject)

    The colorful, glass **marbles** **spilled** onto the floor.

                  marbles **spilled**

In the following exercise match a subject with a predicate, so that each sentence makes sense.

Subject

4. Aqueducts F
5. The moon C
6. The loosely-woven curtains G
7. Everyone at the surprise party A
8. Grasshoppers H
9. Fireworks B
10. The audience D
11. The Hopi Indians E

Predicate

A. brought a funny gift.
B. explode with noise and color.
C. cast a bright light on the snow.
D. applauded long after the curtain came down.
E. live in the Arizona desert.
F. were built by the Romans to carry water.
G. hung unevenly.
H. do great damage to crops.

The Compound Sentence

A **compound** sentence consists of two simple sentences that are joined by a conjunction such as **and, but, or**. In each of the compound sentences that follow, the simple sentences are underlined. A comma is used before each conjunction.

<u>The band started playing</u>, and <u>everyone got up to dance.</u>

<u>The band started playing</u>, but <u>only a few people got up to dance.</u>

<u>Would you rather dance</u>, or <u>do you prefer to listen to the music?</u>

In exercises 12-14, do the following:

- Underline each of the two simple sentences.
- Circle the conjunction that connects these sentences.
- Place the comma where it belongs.

I can come to the party and I'll bring a cake.

12. _____

I will help you with your work later but I want to rest now.

13. _____

Do you want to eat at eleven or would you rather eat at twelve?

14. _____

The Complete Sentence

The Complex Sentence

A **complex** sentence consists of a **subordinate clause** (a fragment) and a **main clause** (which can stand alone as a complete sentence). In other words, a complex sentence is made up of an incomplete thought and a complete thought joined together. In each of the complex sentences below, underline the subordinate clause once and the main clause twice. The first one is done for you.

If I plan ahead, I can achieve all my goals.

15. When you leave the room, please close the door quietly.
16. If I can borrow a car, I am going to the beach.
17. When I swim, I like to wear goggles.
18. While we're on vacation, my brother and I plan to go sailing.

When a complex sentence begins with a subordinate clause, you need to use a comma.

When the main clause comes first and the subordinate clause second, no comma is needed. In each of the complex sentences below underline the main clause twice and the subordinate clause once. The first one is done for you.

I can achieve all my goals if I plan ahead.

19. Please close the door quietly when you leave the room.
20. I am going to the beach if I can borrow a car.
21. I like to wear goggles when I swim.
22. My brother and I plan to go sailing while we're on vacation.

You do not need to use a comma when a complex sentence begins with a main clause.

Sentence Fragments

A group of words that does not express a complete idea is called a **sentence fragment**. A fragment is only a part of something. When you read a fragment, you know that words are missing.

    The woman brushing her hair

Below are some of the ways this fragment can be made into a complete sentence.

    The woman is brushing her hair.
    The woman brushing her hair is pretty.
    I saw the woman brushing her hair.
    Is the woman brushing her hair?

Rewrite the two fragments below so that each expresses a complete thought in a complete sentence.

23. The students washing cars
24. An artist painting the sunrise

Run-on Sentences

While the sentence fragment leaves things out, the run-on sentence combines ideas that should be separated. A run-on sentence occurs when two or more sentences are written as one. Several ideas that all seem to run together are presented at once, making it difficult for the reader to understand what the writer is trying to say. The following is an example of a run-on sentence.

On my way to work I got a flat tire but I didn't have the tools to change it myself so I tied a white cloth to the antenna and waited inside my car until finally a passing motorist stopped when he noticed the white cloth and offered to change the tire for me even though he was in a hurry he stopped because he is an individual who cares about other people.

In the passage above there are far too many ideas to fit into one sentence. You can correct run-on sentences with proper end punctuation, conjunctions, or semicolons.

End Punctuation

The kind of end punctuation you use in your writing depends upon the purpose of your sentence. A **declarative** sentence, making a statement, ends in a period. An **imperative** sentence that makes a demand or a request also ends in a period. An **interrogative** sentence asks a question and ends with a question mark. An **exclamatory** sentence, which is used to express strong feeling, ends with an exclamation point.

    declarative: *My car has a flat tire.*
    imperative: *Please fix my flat tire for me.*
    interrogative: *Can you fix that flat tire?*
    exclamatory: *Oh no, my car has another flat!*

The Conjunction

The conjunction is a word that is used to connect two complete thoughts. The following words are conjunctions: **and, but, or**. In the example below, two thoughts are connected by the conjunction *but*.

    I would have helped change the tire, **but**

    I didn't have time to stop.

In the following exercise, connect each pair of sentences with the most appropriate conjunction: and, but, or. Remember to use a comma (,) before each conjunction.

My car has a flat tire. I may have to walk to work.

25. _____

I would have changed the tire. I didn't have the tools to do it.

26. _____

Can you change the tire? Do you want to call the service station?

27. _____

The Semicolon

A semicolon (;) is used to connect two related sentences when they are not joined by a conjunction. A semicolon can be used in place of a conjunction. The first word that follows a semicolon begins with a lower case (small) letter.

> **Conjunction**   He cares about other people, **and** he always offers to help.
>
> **Semicolon**   He cares about other people; he always offers to help.

Use a semicolon to connect each set of sentences below.

She waited by the side of the road. Many cars passed by without stopping.

28. _____

He saw a white cloth tied to the radio antenna. He knew she needed help.

29. _____

The man was kind. He changed the tire.

30. _____

Score the Practice exercise using the Answer Key, and go on to the Composition part of this guide.

Composition

This part of the guide will help you apply what you have learned about writing complete sentences. Read the run-on sentence that follows.

On my way to work I got a flat tire but I didn't have the tools to change it myself so I tied a white cloth to the antenna and waited inside my car until finally a passing motorist stopped when he noticed the white cloth and offered to change the tire for me even though he was in a hurry he stopped because he is an individual who cares about other people.

Follow the steps outlined here to correct the run-on sentence.

- Rewrite the passage so that it contains complete sentences that present all of the writer's ideas.

- Use any of the ways you have learned, alone or in combination, to correct the run-on sentence. You may want to add or eliminate some words.

Use the Checklist to help you review and revise your writing. Do this for all drafts and your final copy.

Checklist   Yes   No

1. I rewrote the passage so that it contains only complete sentences.   ____ ____

2. I used capital letters to begin each sentence.   ____ ____

3. I used proper end punctuation for each sentence.   ____ ____

4. I used commas and conjunctions to combine my ideas.   ____ ____

5. I used the semicolon to connect two sentences that are closely related in thought.   ____ ____

6. I proofread and edited my writing.   ____ ____
   Proofread: to look for errors and indicate them.
   Edit: to revise your writing, if necessary.

7. I wrote a corrected copy of my work.   ____ ____

Submit the completed writing assignment and Practice exercise to your instructor for evaluation.

Answering Questions

This guide will help you to answer questions clearly and completely. Answering questions in writing can prove to be a very valuable skill in school, at work, and in your personal correspondence. There are **three** important rules to remember when answering a question.

- Use complete sentences to answer the question.

- Restate the entire question in your answer so that the reader knows all parts of the question.

- Provide information from the reading selection. If the question is not based on a reading, draw on your own knowledge and experience to answer the question. You may want to use a reference source such as an encyclopedia.

Read the following passage from "The Scarlet Ibis," a short story by James Hurst. The story is about a boy and his sickly baby brother.

> When he was two, if you laid him on his stomach, he began to try to move himself, straining terribly. The doctor said that with his weak heart this strain would probably kill him, but it didn't. Trembling, he'd push himself up, turning first red, then a soft purple, and finally collapse back onto the bed like an old worn-out doll. I can still see Mama watching him, her hand pressed tight across her mouth, her eyes wide and unblinking. But he learned to crawl (it was his third winter), and we brought him out of the front bedroom, putting him on the rug before the fireplace. For the first time he became one of us.

Practice

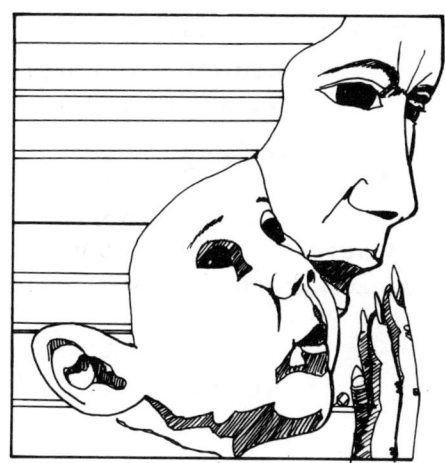

Read each part of the following exercise and answer all **18** questions. For each item, write either **yes** or **no**.

Question Why is the mother scared as she watches her baby straining to move?

Written below are three different answers to this question. Read each answer and complete the exercise that follows it.

Answer Because the doctor has said it would kill him.

1. _____ Is this answer a complete sentence?

2. _____ Does the answer restate the entire question?

3. _____ Does the answer provide information from the reading selection?

Answer The doctor said that the straining would kill him.

4. _____ Is this answer a complete sentence?

5. _____ Does the answer restate the entire question?

6. _____ Does the answer provide information from the reading selection?

Answer The mother is scared as she watches her baby straining to move, because the doctor has said that the strain on his weak heart would probably kill the child.

7. _____ Is this answer a complete sentence?

8. _____ Does the answer restate the entire question?

9. _____ Does the answer provide information from the reading selection?

In this next part there are three questions. Each is followed by a group of answers. Only one answer in each group conforms to the three rules for answering questions:

The answer is a complete sentence

The answer restates the entire question.

The answer provides information from the reading selection, or from your own knowledge and experience.

Write **yes** for those answers that comply with all three rules. Write **no** for those answers that do not comply with all three rules.

Question Why is the sky blue?

10. _____ Because of dust particles and water vapor in our atmosphere.

11. _____ It reflects only blue.

12. _____ The sky is blue because dust particles and water vapor in our atmosphere reflect only blue.

Question Why would someone say that a mirror is truthful?

13. _____ Someone would say that a mirror is truthful because it makes us see ourselves as we really are.

14. _____ Because it makes us see ourselves.

15. _____ It's truthful because it makes us see ourselves as we really are.

Question Why is ice cream delicious on a hot summer day?

16. _____ It tastes good and is so refreshing.

17. _____ Because it's so refreshing.

18. _____ Ice cream is delicious on a hot summer day because it tastes good and is so refreshing.

Score the Practice exercise using the Answer Key, and go on to the Composition part of this guide.

Composition

This part of the guide will help you apply what you have learned about answering questions. Choose a fiction or nonfiction selection to read from available textbooks. Check to see that the selection is followed by *thought* or *review* questions about the reading. After you read the selection, do the following:

- Copy **five** questions and answer each, keeping in mind the three rules you have learned.

Use the Checklist to help you review and revise your writing. Do this for all drafts and your final copy.

Checklist   Yes   No

1. I selected five questions and answered all of them.   ____   ____

2. My answers conform to the three rules for answering questions.   ____   ____

3. I used capital letters to begin each sentence, and proper end punctuation.   ____   ____

4. I used commas and conjunctions to combine my ideas.   ____   ____

5. I proofread and edited my writing.   ____   ____
   Proofread: to look for errors and indicate them.
   Edit: to revise your writing, if necessary.

6. I wrote a corrected copy of my work.   ____   ____

Submit the completed writing assignment and Practice exercise to your instructor for evaluation.

Transitional Words and Phrases

This guide will help you to use transitional words and phrases. **When you want to connect two ideas in writing, transitions act as links that hold your ideas together.** The links you wish to make in your writing depend on your purpose. Below are a series of exercises in which transitional words and phrases are used.

Practice

Read each part of the following exercise and answer all **28** questions.

Time Relationships

In a time relationship events can occur before, at the same time as, or after other events.

> **Example** A rainbow appeared **after** the rain.

If your purpose is to show a time relationship, the words below will help you. Choose words from this list to fill in the blanks in the two paragraphs that follow.

after	eventually	later	soon
afterwards	finally	meanwhile	sooner
always	first	next	so that
as soon as	following	now	then
at the same time	immediately	once	today
before	in order to	second	until
during	in the meantime	someday	when
earlier	last	sometimes	

23

Transitional Words and Phrases

The alarm clock rings. _____ I get out of bed. I prepare my clothes _____ I wash up. I get dressed, and _____ I eat breakfast. _____ I'm ready to leave. Today looks like it's going to be a fine day.

Let's make dinner. _____ make salad. _____ broil the steaks. Don't let them burn. _____ set the table. _____ pour the wine. Enjoy!

Relationships Between Ideas

When you want to express two related thoughts about the same subject, you can connect them using transitions.

Example   Today is a great day **because** I got the job I wanted.

If your purpose is to show a relationship between ideas, the words below will help you. Choose words from this list to fill in the blanks in the two paragraphs that follow.

accordingly	even though	mainly	similarly
also	furthermore	moreover	since
and	if	more important	therefore
as	in the same way	most important	unless
because	like	nevertheless	while
besides	likewise	otherwise	

You can make your dreams come true, _____9_____ you want them to. _____10_____ you are young, you can begin to make plans. You will succeed _____11_____ you have a direction and goals.

A good education and practical experience are often the keys to success. _____12_____ formal education is important, on the job experience is _____13_____ needed. You will be a more confident _____14_____ poised applicant _____15_____ you are sure of your skills.

Restating Main Ideas

When you restate an idea, you say the same thing another way.

Example The facts show that regular exercise is good for your health. **As a result**, millions of people have started jogging, swimming, and dancing.

If your purpose is to restate main ideas, the words below will help you. Choose words from this list to fill in the blanks in the two paragraphs that follow.

Transitional Words and Phrases

as a result	consequently	hence	since
as a result of	due to	in conclusion	so
as long as	evidently	in view of	summarily
because of	for this reason	it is evident	thus

Drinking and driving don't mix. _____(16)_____ alcohol slows your reflexes and clouds your judgment, driving while drunk can be dangerous. _____(17)_____ all of the alcohol related injuries and deaths, many states impose severe penalties for driving while intoxicated. _____(18)_____, to protect your own life and the lives of others, drive sober.

The dollar buys less today _____(19)_____ inflation. _____(20)_____, people must buy carefully. _____(21)_____, a penny saved is a penny earned.

Opposite Points of View

You can use transitions to connect two opposing ideas.

> **Example** Travel by train is interesting, **but** flying is faster.

If your purpose is to express opposite points of view, the words below will help you. Choose words from this list to fill in the blanks in the two paragraphs that follow.

although	in contrast	the reverse	while
but	on the contrary	though	yet
conversely	on the other hand	unless	
however	than	unlike	

The thought of living on your own sounds exciting, _____22_____ it may not be so easy to do. _____23_____ the freedom of making your own choices is tempting, earning money and keeping a house can be difficult. Many young people think about living alone, _____24_____ actually doing it requires a lot of planning. _____25_____ you are really ready, think twice about going out on your own.

Sharing an apartment with others has both good and bad points. Sharing expenses can be a real advantage, _____26_____ only if people cooperate. It is comforting to have people around. _____27_____, there are times when you want to be alone. When you live by yourself, you don't have to be concerned with what your roommates think or feel. Don't plan to live with others _____28_____ you are prepared to make compromises.

There are many other transitional words and phrases besides the ones mentioned here. All transitions act as links that connect ideas and create unity in your writing. The list of transitions at the back of this book is for your reference when you write.

Score the Practice exercise using the Answer Key, and go on to Composition part of this guide.

Transitional Words and Phrases

Composition

This part of the guide will help you apply what you have learned about using transitional words and phrases. For each of the four exercises, follow these steps:

- Refer to the lists of transitions in the Practice exercise or at the back of this book to help you.
- Underline transitional words and phrases that you use in your writing.

1. Choose one topic and write **three** sentences that show time relationships.

Sunday morning	getting ready for a date
the end of the day	stages in a person's life

2. Choose one topic and write **three** sentences that show relationships between ideas.

after graduation	household chores
sharing feelings	old age

3. State the main idea of the topic you wrote about in exercise number two. Then write **two** sentences that restate this idea.

4. Choose one topic and write **three** sentences that express opposite points of view.

school prayer	teenage marriage
the drinking age	country vs. city living

Use the Checklist to help you review and revise your writing. Do this for all drafts and your final copy.

Checklist   Yes   No

1. I wrote three sentences that use transitional words and phrases to show time relationships.   ____ ____

2. I wrote three sentences that use transitional words and phrases to show relationships between ideas.   ____ ____

3. I wrote two sentences that use transitional words and phrases to restate a main idea.   ____ ____

4. I wrote three sentences that use transitional words and phrases to present opposite points of view.   ____ ____

5. I wrote complete sentences.   ____ ____

6. I used capital letters to begin each sentence, and proper end punctuation.   ____ ____

7. I proofread and edited my writing.   ____ ____
   Proofread: to look for errors and indicate them.
   Edit: to revise your writing, if necessary.

8. I wrote a corrected copy of my work.   ____ ____

Submit the completed writing assignment and Practice exercise to your instructor for evaluation.

Combining Sentences

This guide will help you to combine sentences in your writing. While ideas can be stated one by one, in separate short sentences (**kernels**), your writing will be more interesting and effective if you combine these sentences. As with transitional words and phrases, you can use sentence combining to connect ideas and create unity in your writing.

Practice

Read each part of the following exercise and answer all **22** questions. Begin by reading the model paragraph.

It is a Sunday afternoon in early autumn. The day is perfect for taking a stroll through the park. Leaves fall from the trees, covering the ground with many colors. A young couple hold hands as they walk by. Their sparkling eyes reflect the sun's brilliant rays. The day is like a painting that is alive with people and colors.

The sentences below are from the model paragraph. Each sentence, containing several ideas, is further reduced to kernel sentences. A kernel sentence presents only one idea about the subject.

A group of related kernel sentences is called a cluster. The **base** sentence of the cluster conveys the essential fact or idea being expressed, while the other sentences provide information that helps to describe or explain the main idea. The base sentence in each cluster below is indicated in parentheses.

Answer the cluster of questions that follow each sentence from the paragraph. Fill in each blank with one word to make a kernel sentence. These kernels are the building blocks of the more complex sentences that appear in the model.

It is a Sunday afternoon in early autumn.

   What day of the week is it?

1. It is _____ . (base sentence)

   What time of day is it?

2. It is _____ .

   What season of the year is it?

3. It is _____ .

   What part of the season is it?

4. It is _____ autumn.

Kernel sentences 1, 2, 3, and 4, when combined, make the first sentence of the paragraph.

Combining Sentences

The day is perfect for taking a stroll through the park.

    What kind of day is it?

5. It is a _____ day. (base sentence)

    What is the day perfect for doing?

6. The day is perfect for taking a _____ .

    Where does the stroll take place?

7. The stroll is through the _____ .

Kernel sentences 5, 6, and 7, when combined, make the second sentence of the paragraph.

Leaves fall from the trees, covering the ground with many colors.

    What falls?

8. The _____ fall. (base sentence)

    Where do they fall from?

9. Leaves fall from the _____ .

    What are the leaves doing to the ground?

10. The leaves are _____ the ground.

    How do the leaves differ from one another?

11. The leaves are of many _____ .

Kernel sentences 8, 9, 10, and 11, when combined, make the third sentence of the paragraph.

A young couple hold hands as they walk by.

    Who walks by?

12. A _____ walks by. (base sentence)

    How old are they?

13. They are _____ .

    What are they doing?

14. They are _____ .

Kernel sentences 12, 13, and 14, when combined, make the fourth sentence of the paragraph.

Their sparkling eyes reflect the sun's brilliant rays.

    What kind of eyes do they have?

15. They have _____ eyes.

    What do their eyes reflect?

16. Their eyes reflect _____ . (base sentence)

    Where are the rays from?

17. The rays are from the _____ .

    What kind of rays are they?

18. They are _____ rays.

Kernel sentences 15, 16, 17, and 18, when combined, make the fifth sentence of the paragraph.

The day is like a painting that is alive with people and colors.

    What is the day like?

19. The day is like a _____ . (base sentence)

    What is special about the painting?

20. This painting is _____ .

    What is alive in the painting?

21. _____ are alive in the painting.

    What else is alive in the painting?

22. _____ are alive in the painting.

Kernel sentences 19, 20, 21, and 22, when combined, make the last sentence of the paragraph.

Score the Practice exercise using the Answer Key, and go on to the Composition part of this guide.

Composition

This part of the guide will help you apply what you have learned about sentence combining. Now that you have learned to identify kernels and understand how they may be combined, complete the exercises below from *Sentence Combining* titled Matchstick, Table, Working Girl, and Orchard.

In each exercise, kernel sentences are grouped together in clusters by subject. These simple sentences, each containing a significant detail about the subject, can be combined to make one, more interesting sentence. By completing the following activities, you will become adept at structuring sentences and presenting ideas clearly in writing.

For each exercise do the following:

- Identify the base sentence in each cluster.
- Underline the important information in each kernel sentence.
- Combine the underlined information in each cluster to expand the base sentence. To do this, add, delete, substitute, or rearrange words and phrases. The first cluster is done for you.
- Write each combined sentence, one following the other, to form a paragraph.

MATCHSTICK

1. The <u>match</u> is <u>scraped against the box</u>. (base sentence)
The <u>scraping</u> is a <u>noise</u>.
The noise is <u>raspy</u>.

The match scrapes against the box making a raspy noise.
You might think of other ways to combine these kernel sentences.

2. It sputters into flame.
   The sputtering is uneasy.
   The flame is yellowish.

3. The flame wavers.
   The flame trails its way.
   The way is up the matchstick.

4. Then it dies.
   Its death is with a sudden puff.

5. A wisp threads upward.
   The wisp is smoke.
   The wisp becomes part of the shadows.

TABLE

1. The table is littered with refuse.
   The refuse belongs to other people.

2. They have left signatures everywhere.
   The signatures are stained.
   The signatures are greasy.

3. He stares at cups.
   The cups are in a pile.
   The cups are for coffee.
   The cups are stained with lipstick.

4. Off to one side is a hamburger.
   The hamburger is half-eaten.
   Flies rest there.
   The flies are nervous.

5. The sign is buried in the garbage.
   The sign is small.
   The sign is neatly lettered.

6. He reads the sign.
   The sign pleads for students to bus their own dishes.

WORKING GIRL

1. Jan is a working girl.
   She bounces through a routine.
   The routine is from 8 to 5.

2. Then she waits for the bus.
   The bus takes her back.
   The bus takes her to her apartment.
   The apartment is uptown.

3. She is now on her own.
   She is having a great time.

4. Her senses are alive to something.
   The something is new.
   The something is delicious.
   The something is called "freedom."

5. Each day is electric.
   Each day is exciting.

6. Her face is poised.
   Her face is proud.
   Her face smiles with confidence.
   The confidence is quiet.

7. She has legs.
   Her legs are long.
   Her legs are waxy.

8. She has dates.
   The dates are many.
   But she is in no hurry.
   The hurry would be to settle down.

ORCHARD

1. The orchard was behind the house.
   The house belonged to a grandfather.
   The grandfather was mine.

2. It was a place to visit.
   The place was a favorite.
   The visiting was in the fall.
   The visiting was after school.

3. The trees stood in rows.
   The trees were gnarled.

4. You were alone.
   You could listen to the bees.
   The bees worked.

5. Apples were there.
   They hung from the boughs.
   They were ready for picking.
   They were ready for eating.

6. The air was sweet.
   The air was heavy.
   It smelled of fruit.
   The fruit was ripe.
   The fruit would soon be rotting.

7. Juice would run down your chin.
   You would wipe it.
   The juice was from an apple.
   The wiping was with a sleeve.

8. Then you would notice the leaves.
   The leaves were turning.
   The turning was brown.
   The turning was golden.

Use the Checklist to help you review and revise your writing. Do this for all drafts and your final copy.

Checklist   Yes   No

1. I identified the base sentence in each
   cluster.   ____   ____

2. I underlined the important information in
   each kernel sentence.   ____   ____

3. I combined information in each cluster to
   expand the base sentence.   ____   ____

4. For each exercise, I wrote a series of
   complete sentences that form a paragraph.   ____   ____

5. I used capital letters to begin each
   sentence, and proper end punctuation.   ____   ____

6. I proofread and edited my writing.   ____   ____

   Proofread: to look for errors and indicate them.
   Edit: to revise your writing, if necessary.

7. I wrote a corrected copy of my work.   ____   ____

Submit the completed writing assignment and Practice exercise to you instructor for evaluation.

39

Combining Sentences

Expanding Sentences

This guide will help you to expand sentences in your writing. In the last lesson you learned how to fit several ideas into one sentence to make it more interesting. Sentence expanding, like sentence combining, helps you to add meaning to a simple sentence. When we expand a sentence, we make it more interesting by offering detailed information about who, what, where, when, and why.

Practice

A simple sentence can be expanded by adding adjectives, adverbs, and prepositional phrases. Read the simple sentence and the expanded version that follows:

The canary sings.

The small, yellow canary sings sweetly in his cage.

The **subject** of both sentences is the *canary*, a **noun**. In the second sentence, the **pronoun** *his* replaces this noun. In the expanded sentence, the words *small* and *yellow* tell us something about the canary. Words that describe a noun (person, place, thing, or idea) are called **adjectives**.

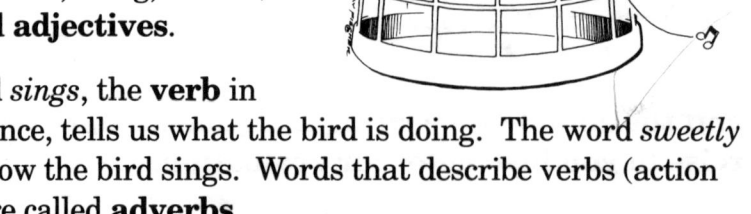

The word *sings*, the **verb** in the sentence, tells us what the bird is doing. The word *sweetly* tells us how the bird sings. Words that describe verbs (action words) are called **adverbs**.

The words *in his cage*, a **prepositional phrase**, tell us where the canary is. Prepositions are words that identify place (*in*, near), direction (*toward, from*), time (*after, until*) or condition (*of, without*). They combine with nouns (*cage*) or pronouns (*his*) to form prepositional phrases. These words or phrases function as transitions in writing.

Now you will have an opportunity to practice what you have just learned about the sentence. Below is a list of parts of speech and their abbreviations, followed by **15** sentences. Identify the parts of speech for the words in each sentence. The first one is done for you. If necessary, refer to the definitions below as you complete the exercise.

noun (*n*) person, place, thing, or idea
pronoun (*pron*) takes the place of a noun. Some examples are:
  I, we, you, she, he, it, they, ours, hers, me, him, them
subject (*subj*) what or who the the sentence is mainly about
adjective (*adj*) a word that describes a noun
verb (*vb*) an action word
adverb (*adv*) describes an action word
prepositional phrase (*prep phrase*) identifies place, time, or
  condition and begins with words such as: *in, near, toward,
  from, after, until, of, without*

1. The hungry hikers quickly devoured the delicious meal and sang songs in front of the campfire.

hungry:	adj
hikers:	subj (n)
quickly:	adv
devoured:	vb
delicious:	adj
meal:	n
sang:	vb
songs:	n
in front of the campfire:	prep. phrase
campfire:	n

Expanding Sentences

2. The young women, wearing straw hats and flowered shawls, proudly prepared for the festivities.

   young:
   women:
   wearing:
   straw:
   hats:
   flowered:
   shawls:
   proudly:
   prepared:
   for the festivities:
   festivities:

3. Every October, thousands of grey whales leave the Chukchi Sea in search of warmer waters.

   Every:
   October:
   thousands:
   grey:
   whales:
   leave:
   Chukchi Sea:
   in search of warmer waters:
   warmer:
   waters:

4. The large, green bullfrog croaked loudly, then splashed into the water.

   large:
   green:
   bullfrog:
   croaked:
   loudly:

splashed:
into the water:
water:

5. The holiday crowd waited restlessly for the fireworks to begin.

holiday:
crowd:
waited:
restlessly:
for the fireworks to begin:
fireworks:
begin:

6. Along the creek, a small grey and black raccoon drank the cool water and daintily washed his furry paws.

along the creek:
creek:
small:
grey:
black:
raccoon:
drank:
cool:
water:
daintily:
washed:
furry:
paws:

7. The stream swirled lazily over mossy rocks and wooden logs before it emptied into a lake.

stream:
swirled:
lazily:

Expanding Sentences

over mossy rocks and wooden logs:
mossy:
rocks:
wooden:
logs:
before it emptied into a lake:
emptied:
lake:

8. The young runner raced aggressively to win first place.

   young:
   runner:
   raced:
   aggressively:
   to win first place:
   win:
   first:
   place:

9. We happily roasted marshmallows over an open fire.

   We:
   happily:
   roasted:
   marshmallows:
   over an open fire:
   open:
   fire:

10. The mountains are clothed in blue and purple because of the angle of the sun in the sky.

    mountains:
    clothed:
    in blue and purple:
    blue:

purple:
because of the angle of the sun:
angle:
sun:
in the sky:
sky:

11. She climbed up into the dark, dusty attic and cautiously explored its contents.

    She:
    climbed:
    up into the dark, dusty attic:
    dark:
    dusty:
    attic:
    cautiously:
    explored:
    contents:

12. In one closet of the old mansion hung threadbare, wool coats with fur collars and velvet lapels.

    In one closet:
    one:
    closet:
    of the old mansion:
    hung:
    threadbare:
    wool:
    coats:
    with fur collars and velvet lapels:
    fur:
    collars:
    velvet:
    lapels:

13. The woods were already filled with shadows, though a bright sunset still glimmered faintly among the trunks of the trees.

    woods:
    already:
    filled:
    shadows:
    bright:
    sunset:
    still:
    glimmered:
    faintly:
    among the trunks of the trees:
    trunks:
    trees:

14. At the edge of the cliff stood a lighthouse, its beacon constantly circling in the night.

    At the edge of the cliff:
    edge:
    cliff:
    stood:
    lighthouse:
    beacon:
    constantly:
    circling:
    in the night:
    night:

15. The chocolate pudding was placed on the table beside the luscious, freshly whipped cream.

    chocolate:
    pudding:
    placed:
    on the table:

table:
beside the luscious, freshly whipped cream:
luscious:
freshly:
whipped:
cream:

Score the Practice exercise using the Answer Key, and go on to the Composition part of this guide.

Composition

This part of the guide will help you apply what you have learned about expanding sentences. In the exercises that follow, expand each simple sentence by adding significant details about the subject. The questions in parentheses are prompts for writing nouns, adjectives, verbs, adverbs, or prepositional phrases. By completing the following activities, you will become more adept at writing interesting and meaningful sentences.

As you expand each simple sentence you will be:

- describing the subject.
- telling what the subject is doing.
- describing these actions.
- using prepositional phrases to show place, direction, time, or condition.

1. She sat down (*how*) (*where*) and (*did what*) her face with (*what*).

2. As Marie reached (*what*) she saw the lights (*doing what*) (*where*) like a host of stars.

3. It took (*how many*) (*what kind*) days to (*do what*) the (*what kind*) mountains before (*who*) could rest.

4. One by one the (*who*) moved (*how*) past the (*what kind*) barbed wire and began to (*do what*) (*where*).

5. He lies back in his (*what*) (*does what*) his eyes and imagines he grew up in a house (*where*) surrounded by (*what*) (*what kind*).

6. I grew up (*where*) at Grandma's listening (*how*) from behind her rocking chair as she and (*who*) talked about (*what*).

7. (*when*) that evening they walked (*how*) (*where*) under (*what*) listening to the (*what kind*) sound of the crickets.

8. Most popcorn chewers at (*where*) stop (*doing what*) momentarily just before the (*what*).

9. (*when*) the animals search (*how*) for food in order to (*do what*) until (*when*).

10. (*how many*) areas which were once covered with (*what*) have turned into (*what kind*) land where the soil is (*how*) and looks like (*what*).

Use the Checklist to help you review and revise your writing. Do this for all drafts and your final copy.

Checklist	**Yes**	**No**

1. I expanded each simple sentence by adding significant details about the subject. _____ _____

2. I added nouns, adjectives, verbs, adverbs, and prepositional phrases where appropriate. _____ _____

3. I described subjects, their actions, and showed relationships between ideas. _____ _____

4. I used capital letters to begin each sentence, and proper end punctuation. _____ _____

5. I proofread and edited my writing. _____ _____
   Proofread: to look for errors and indicate them.
   Edit: to revise your writing, if necessary.

6. I wrote a corrected copy of my work. _____ _____

Submit the completed writing assignment and Practice exercise to your instructor for evaluation.

Paragraph Development

This guide will help you to write a paragraph. A paragraph is composed of three parts:

- a topic sentence
- supporting details
- a concluding sentence

Practice

Read each part of the following exercise and answer all **17** questions. Begin by reading the model paragraph.

> Anyone can build a campfire. You begin with some wood shavings or small dry twigs. On top of that you place some larger twigs or thin branches. When you begin to pile on the heavier wooden pieces, use a crisscross pattern. This leaves plenty of space for the fire to come through. Light the wood shavings or dried twigs with a match, and the job is done. There is nothing complicated about building a campfire.

The **topic sentence** tells the reader what the paragraph is about. It is usually the first sentence. Copy the topic sentence of the paragraph.

1. _____

Supporting details provide facts, examples, and descriptions that relate to the topic of the paragraph. Copy each sentence that presents facts, examples, or descriptions about how to build a campfire.

2. _____
3. _____
4. _____
5. _____
6. _____

The **concluding sentence** summarizes the topic of the paragraph for the reader. Copy the last sentence of the paragraph.

7. _____

Read the following paragraph:

> When I was little, my older sister was always trying to scare me. One night she hid near the bottom of the staircase. As I walked by, she jumped out at me and let loose a loud, bloodcurdling scream. Another time I asked her to tell me a bedtime story. Holding a small flashlight under her chin, she turned the lights off, lowered her voice to a whisper, and opened her eyes wide. I was terrified and she hadn't even started the story! Her tales of ghosts and monsters kept me shivering with fright long after she left the room. Now, I laugh whenever I recall how easily my sister could scare me when I was young.

Copy the topic sentence of the paragraph.

8. _____

Paragraph Development

List **three** ways the older sister scared the young child. These are the supporting details for the topic of the paragraph.

9. _____
10. _____
11. _____

Copy the concluding sentence of the paragraph.

12. _____

Read the following paragraph:

When I looked through our family photo album last Sunday, I was reminded of all the good times we had during our summer vacations. There were several photos of Dad and me in a boat, holding our prize catches for the day. I saw five pictures I took of my sister learning to water ski. Most of the time she was in the water. The funniest picture was a closeup of my family as we rode the Water Flume at an amusement park. Mom looked as if she were about to be shot. The photographer knew exactly when to snap that one! Summer vacations are great because I always have a wonderful time.

Copy the topic sentence of the paragraph

13. _____

List **three** different vacation activities mentioned in the paragraph. These are the supporting details for the topic of this paragraph.

14. _____

15. _____

16. _____

Copy the concluding sentence of the paragraph.

17. _____

Score the Practice exercise using the Answer Key, and go on to the Composition part of this guide.

Composition

This part of the guide will help you apply what you have learned about writing a paragraph. Choose **one** topic and write a paragraph. Follow the plan outlined below.

Topics

If I had only a year to live . . .

The best friend I ever had . . .

I was once punished for . . .

When I was little, I was really afraid of . . .

The funniest experience I ever had . . .

Plan

- Indent to indicate the beginning of the paragraph. Introduce your topic in the first sentence.

- Write at least **five** sentences that contain supporting details: facts, examples, and descriptions that relate to the topic.

- Write a concluding statement that summarizes the topic of the paragraph for the reader.

Use the Checklist to help you review and revise your writing. Do this for all drafts and your final copy.

Checklist   Yes   No

1. I indented to begin my paragraph.   ____   ____

2. I introduced my topic in the first sentence.   ____   ____

3. I wrote at least five sentences that contain supporting details for my topic.   ____   ____

4. The last sentence of the paragraph summarizes the topic for the reader.   ____   ____

5. I used transitions to connect ideas and create unity in my writing.   ____   ____

6. I wrote complete sentences that begin with capital letters, and used proper end punctuation.   ____   ____

7. I proofread and edited my composition.   ____   ____

8. I wrote a corrected copy of my work.   ____   ____

Submit the completed writing assignment and Practice exercise to your instructor for evaluation.

The Narrative Paragraph

This guide will help you to write a narrative paragraph. **A narrative tells a story.** The model paragraph is from "An Ornery Kind of Kid," a short story by William Saroyan.

Practice

Read each part of the following exercise and answer all **13** questions. Begin by reading the paragraph.

> It was getting dark fast by then, and there didn't seem to be anything alive around at all, so he began to shoot the gun just to get used to it. Pretty soon he could shoot it and not get knocked down. He kept shooting and walking, and finally it was dark and it seemed he was lost. He stumbled over a hidden rock and fell and shot the gun by accident and got a lot of dirt in his eyes. He got up and almost cried, but he managed not to, and then he found a road, but he had no idea where it went or which direction to take. He was scratched and sore all over and not very happy about the way he'd shot the gun by accident. He was scared, too, and he said a prayer a minute and meant every word of what he said. And he understood for the first time in his life why people liked to go to church.

The author begins by creating the setting. The setting tells the reader the **time** and **place** of the story. He then tells what happens to a specific character. We can use all the information in the paragraph to make inferences (draw conclusions) in answering the questions.

1. Use the dictionary to find the definition of the word *ornery*.

2. What time of day is it?

3. What words in the paragraph help you to draw this conclusion?

4. Where does the story take place?

5. What words in the paragraph help you to draw this conclusion?

6. Is the author writing about an adult or a young person?
   _____

7. What words in the paragraph help you to draw this conclusion?
   _____

8. What is the character doing?
   _____

9. What words in the paragraph help you to draw this conclusion.
   _____

10. How does the character feel?
    _____

11. What words in the paragraph help you to draw this conclusion?
    _____

12. How does the character in this paragraph console himself?
    _____

13. What words in the paragraph help you to draw this conclusion?
    _____

Score the exercise using the Answer Key, and go on to the Composition part of this guide.

The Narrative Paragraph

Composition

This part of the guide will help you apply what you have learned about writing a narrative paragraph. Choose **one** topic and list, in chronological order, the things that happened. Use this list as you follow the plan for writing a narrative paragraph.

Topics

The first time I went on a date.

The first time I took a ride on a rollercoaster.

The first time I traveled alone.

The last time I had an accident.

The last time I got blamed, and it wasn't my fault.

Plan

- Begin your paragraph by creating the setting. The setting tells the reader the time and place of the story.

- You are the narrator of this story. Tell who you are and what is happening in the story. Choose your details carefully, using words that create a picture for the reader. Write at least **five** sentences for this part.

- Write **two** sentences to end your paragraph. Tell the reader **how** you feel about the outcome, and **why** you feel this way.

Use the Checklist to help you review and revise your writing. Do this for all drafts and your final copy.

Checklist   Yes   No

1. Before I began my paragraph, I listed the
   things that happened in chronological order.   ____   ____

2. I began the paragraph by creating the setting.   ____   ____

3. I told what happened, in detail. I wrote at
   least five sentences for this part.   ____   ____

4. In my concluding sentences, I expressed my
   feelings about the outcome.   ____   ____

5. I used transitions to connect ideas and create
   unity in my writing.   ____   ____

6. I wrote complete sentences that begin with
   capital letters, and used proper end
   punctuation.   ____   ____

7. I proofread and edited my composition.   ____   ____

8. I wrote a corrected copy of my work.   ____   ____

Submit the completed writing assignment and Practice exercise to your instructor for evaluation.

The Descriptive Paragraph

This guide will help you to write a descriptive paragraph. Description is used to create impressions that are vivid, real, and lifelike for the reader.

The writer appeals to the **five senses** by telling us how something **looks**, **tastes**, **smells**, **sounds**, and **feels**. These are five ways of describing a person, place, thing, or idea.

Practice

Read the model paragraph from "A Sound of Thunder" by Ray Bradbury, and answer all **45** questions.

> It came on great oiled striding legs. It towered thirty feet above half the trees, a great evil god. Each lower leg was a piston, a thousand pounds of white bone and thick ropes of muscle. Each thigh was a ton of meat. And from the upper body two delicate arms dangled out front with hands that might pick up men like toys. The snake neck coiled. Its mouth hung open showing a row of teeth like daggers. Its eyes rolled. They showed nothing but hunger. It closed its mouth in a death grin.

The sentences below are from the model paragraph that describes a monster. Each sentence is followed by a list of the five senses, the ways in which we know the world. Write the word(s) from each sentence next to the sensory category to which they belong. If no words from the sentence fit the category, write the word *none*. The first one is done for you.

It came on great oiled striding legs.

sight: **great oiled striding legs**

taste: **none**

smell: **none**

sound: **striding legs**

touch: **oiled**

It towered thirty feet above half the trees, a great evil god.

1. sight: 4. sound:

2. taste: 5. touch:

3. smell:

Each lower leg was a piston, a thousand pounds of white bone and thick ropes of muscle.

6. sight: 9. sound:

7. taste: 10. touch:

8. smell:

61

The Descriptive Paragraph

Each thigh was a ton of meat.

11. sight: 14. sound:

12. taste: 15. touch:

13. smell:

And from the upper body two delicate arms dangled out front with hands that might pick up men like toys.

16. sight: 19. sound:

17. taste: 20. touch:

18. smell:

The snake neck coiled.

21. sight: 24. sound:

22. taste: 25. touch:

23. smell:

Its mouth hung open showing a row of teeth like daggers.

26. sight: 29. sound:

27. taste: 30. touch:

28. smell:

Its eyes rolled.

31. sight: 34. sound:

32. taste: 35. touch:

33. smell:

They showed nothing but hunger.

36. sight: 39. sound:

37. taste: 40. touch:

38. smell:

It closed its mouth in a death grin.

41. sight: 44. sound:

42. taste: 45. touch:

43. smell:

Appealing primarily to the sense of sight, Ray Bradbury has created very vivid impressions for the reader.

Score the exercise using the Answer Key, and go on to the Composition part of this guide.

Composition

This part of the guide will help you apply what you have learned about writing a descriptive paragraph. Choose **one** topic from the group below. List the ways in which your subject appeals to each of the five senses. Use this list to develop your descriptive paragraph. Follow the plan outlined below.

Topics

A dream car

A rock concert

A birthday party

A beautiful sunrise

An outrageous person

Plan

- In the first sentence introduce the person, place, thing, or idea your paragraph is about.

- Write at least **five** sentences in which you describe your subject as completely as possible. Appeal to as many senses as you can: sight, taste, smell, hearing, and touch. The actions of your subject may also be described.

- Write a concluding sentence that uses description to summarize the topic.

Use the Checklist to help you review and revise your writing. Do this for all drafts and your final copy.

Checklist   Yes   No

1. Before I began my paragraph, I listed the ways in which my subject appeals to each of the five senses.   ____ ____

2. In the first sentence I introduced the person, place, thing, or idea my paragraph is about.   ____ ____

3. I described my subject by appealing to the senses. (Check [✓] those that apply):   ____ ____

   sight ____ taste ____ smell ____

   sound ____ touch ____

4. I wrote at least five sentences of description.   ____ ____

5. I wrote a concluding sentence that contains description.   ____ ____

6. I used transitions to connect ideas and create unity in my writing.   ____ ____

7. I wrote complete sentences that begin with capital letters, and used proper end punctuation.   ____ ____

8. I proofread and edited my composition.   ____ ____

9. I wrote a corrected copy of my work.   ____ ____

Submit the completed writing assignment and Practice exercise to your instructor for evaluation.

The Expository Paragraph

This guide will help you to write an expository paragraph. **Exposition** is writing that **explains facts and ideas** so that they are easily understood. You can use expository writing to:

- give directions about how to do something or how to get somewhere.

- explain why something is the way it is.

- write about a person, place, or event, as you might in a research report.

Practice

Read each part of the following exercise and answer all **23** questions.

The sentences on the following page are from the book, *Modern Spearfishing* by I.S. Ivanovic. The sentences have been rearranged so that they are not in the right sequence. In the correct order, these sentences form an expository paragraph. The author uses exposition to give directions about how to prepare for spearfishing.

Reorganize the sentences that follow, A through I, to form a paragraph that clearly explains how one prepares to go spearfishing. First, look for the topic sentence. Next, look for transitional words which serve as clues to the order of the sentences.

Write a **number** next to each sentence to indicate its correct order in the paragraph. For example, write the number 1 next to the sentence which should come first in the paragraph. Use the numbers 2 through 9 to order the remaining sentences.

_____ A. Then place the gun near the edge of the water so that you can pick it up on your way in.

_____ B. You will find it best to make the flippers wet before you try to put them on.

_____ C. Once the goggles are on and your breathing tube is in your mouth, you are ready to go into the water.

_____ D. Put your ear plugs into your ears and put your rubber bathing cap on if you have one.

_____ E. I have found that the following sequence of preparatory steps for spearfishing has proved to be the most useful, although every fisherman develops his own way very soon.

_____ F. The next thing to do is to sit down on the ground, keeping as near to the edge of the water as you can, and then put on your flippers.

_____ G. Then tie your fish ring to your belt so that it is always on your left flank.

_____ H. When you have done that, put your glove on and then you are ready to prepare the mask or the goggles by making sure a mist will not form on the inside of the glass.

The Expository Paragraph

_____ I. First of all, load your gun, apply the safety catch if there is one, check your reel, and check the position of your line.

Now that you have reordered the sentences, write them in your notebook in paragraph form. Compare your work with the model that appears at the end of the Practice exercise.

In the topic sentence, the author gives you information about the **content** and **form** of his paragraph.

10. Content refers to the subject that is discussed. What is the subject of this paragraph? _____

11. The form tells us how the paragraph will be organized. How does the author propose to present the information?
_____

12. How many different steps does the author use in explaining how to prepare for spearfishing? _____

13. How many different transitional words and phrases does the author use in this paragraph to go from one step to the next? _____

Write **ten** transitions used in the expository paragraph.

14. _____   19. _____

15. _____   20. _____

16. _____   21. _____

17. _____   22. _____

18. _____   23. _____

from MODERN SPEARFISHING

I have found that the following sequence of preparatory steps for spearfishing has proved to be the most useful, although every fisherman develops his own way very soon. First of all, load your gun, apply the safety catch if there is one, check your reel, and check the position of your line. Then place the gun near the edge of the water so that you can pick it up on your way in. Put your ear plugs into your ears and put your rubber bathing cap on if you have one. The next thing to do is to sit down on the ground, keeping as near to the edge of the water as you can, and then put on your flippers. You will find it best to make the flippers wet before you try to put them on. Then tie your fish ring to your belt so that it is always on your left flank. When you have done that, put your glove on and then you are ready to prepare the mask or the goggles by making sure a mist will not form on the inside of the glass. Once the goggles are on and your breathing tube is in your mouth, you are ready to go into the water.

Score the Practice exercise using the Answer Key, and go on to the Composition part of this guide.

Composition

This part of the guide will help you apply what you have learned about writing an expository paragraph. Choose **one** topic and list at least five steps, in order, that explain a process. Use this list as you follow the plan for writing an expository paragraph.

You may find it helpful to use reference sources such as the dictionary, encyclopedia, or other books. When you use information from reference sources, do not copy directly from the book. Always use your own words to rephrase what you have read.

Topics

Changing a tire

How a rainbow forms

Making a super banana split

Getting to work or school from where you live

The Wright brothers' first flight

Plan

- Write a topic sentence that introduces your subject (content) and tells how the information will be presented (form).

- Write at least **five** sentences in which you explain your subject as completely as possible.

- Write a conclusion for your paragraph that summarizes the topic for the reader.

Use the Checklist to help you review and revise your writing. Do this for all drafts and your final copy.

Checklist   Yes   No

1. Before I began my paragraph, I listed at least five steps that explain a process.   ____   ____

2. I wrote a topic sentence that introduces my subject and tells how I plan to present the information.   ____   ____

3. Using my own words, I wrote at least five sentences in which I explain my subject to the reader.   ____   ____

4. I wrote a conclusion that summarizes my topic for the reader.   ____   ____

5. I used transitions to connect ideas and create unity in my writing.   ____   ____

6. I wrote complete sentences that begin with capital letters, and used proper end punctuation.   ____   ____

7. I proofread and edited my composition.   ____   ____

8. I wrote a corrected copy of my work.   ____   ____

Submit the completed writing assignment and Practice exercise to your instructor for evaluation.

Using Examples

This guide will help you to write a paragraph using examples. **When you give an example, you point out something that is representative of a category.** The United States of America is an example of the category, *country*. Florida is an example of the category, *state*.

Practice

Read each part of this exercise and answer all **16** questions. The following paragraph is an excerpt from the nonfiction article, "As I Saw the U.S.A." Jan Morris, a British writer, uses examples to illustrate the behavior of Americans.

> Few Americans will walk anywhere if they can help it, either for practical purpose or for pleasure. You can do your banking from your car, without leaving the driving seat, by choosing a bank with a "curbside teller." You can post your letters in postboxes that protrude to the level of your car window. You can watch a film from your car in a "drive-in" cinema. At many stores you can be served in your car. At innumerable restaurants waitresses will hitch trays to the car door, so that you can eat without moving. In Florida there is even a "drive-in" church. There is no more characteristic gesture of American life than the casual rolling-down of a car window and the emergence of a hand, to grasp a hot dog or a theater ticket, a pound of apples or an evening paper, a check book or a soft drink from a roadside stall.

Write the topic sentence of this paragraph.

1. _____

The author uses examples to portray how Americans use their cars, rather than their legs, to go places and do things. List these examples below.

2. _____ 5. _____

3. _____ 6. _____

4. _____ 7. _____

In her concluding statement, the author uses more examples to summarize her point of view. Another way of summarizing this paragraph is to write a sentence that restates the point of view first expressed in the topic sentence.

Example It seems that Americans would rather drive than walk.

73

Using Examples

WORD LIST

angry	disco	Mercedes	scared
aunt	Earth	movie	soccer
basketball	excited	museum	spring
brother	fall	pizza	summer
cheeseburger	Ford	Pluto	tacos
concert	golf	purple	tennis
Corvette	grandmother	sailboat	Toyota
cousin	lipstick	salad	twelve
delighted	Mars	Saturn	winter

Each of the words in the list above is an example of a specific category. Write each word next to its appropriate category.

CATEGORIES

8. cars: _____

9. entertainment: _____

10. feelings: _____

11. food: _____

12. planets: _____

13. relatives: _____

14. seasons: _____

15. sports: _____

16. other: _____

Score the Practice exercise using the Answer Key, and go on to the Composition part of this guide.

Composition

This part of the guide will help you to apply what you have learned about writing a paragraph using examples. Each of the topics below can be used as an introduction to an illustrative paragraph. Before you begin your composition, list examples for the category you have chosen to illustrate. Use this list as you follow the plan for writing a paragraph using examples.

Topics

All kinds of people ride subways and buses.

Summer is a wonderful time of year.

A job is important in many ways.

You can tell a lot about a person by the way he or she eats.

There are many ways to travel.

Plan

- Introduce your topic in the first sentence of the paragraph.

- Write at least **five** sentences containing examples that illustrate the topic.

- Write a concluding sentence that summarizes what you have written.

Use the Checklist to help you review and revise your writing. Do this for all drafts and your final copy.

Checklist   Yes   No

1. Before I began my paragraph, I listed examples for the category (topic) I chose. ____ ____

2. I introduced the topic in the first sentence of the paragraph. ____ ____

3. I wrote five sentences which contain examples that illustrate the topic. ____ ____

4. The last sentence of the paragraph summarizes what I have written. ____ ____

5. I used transitions to connect ideas and create unity in my writing. ____ ____

6. I wrote complete sentences that begin with capital letters, and used proper end punctuation. ____ ____

7. I proofread and edited my composition. ____ ____

8. I wrote a corrected copy of my work. ____ ____

Submit the completed writing assignment and Practice exercise to your instructor for evaluation.

Using Definition

This guide will help you to write a paragraph using definition. The definition of a person, place, thing, or idea involves both description and explanation. While description appeals to the senses and is used by the writer to create impressions, **definition presents facts about the subject**.

Practice

Read each part of the following exercise and answer all **19** questions.

When you buy land, it must be surveyed. A survey defines the limits and boundaries of your property and what it contains. In the same way, **definition explains** your subject to your audience **in very concrete terms**. In the following paragraph, the writer uses concrete terms to define the subject.

> The guitar is a handheld, stringed, musical instrument made of wood. The **body** of the guitar is like a box that has a flat front and back, and is hollow inside. The shape is that of a pear or a figure eight. The circular opening on the front of the guitar is called the **sound hole**. A long piece of wood, the **finger board**, is attached to the body of the guitar. Raised ridges, called **frets**, are spaced along the finger board. **Strings** of nylon or steel are stretched across the sound hole from the **bridge** up to the **tuning pegs** at the end of the finger board. This instrument can be played by pressing the strings against the frets with one hand while strumming the guitar with the other. Instruments similar to the guitar are the banjo, the mandolin, the ukulele, and the violin.

Identify the parts of the guitar as labeled in the illustration. Match each letter with the name of a part.

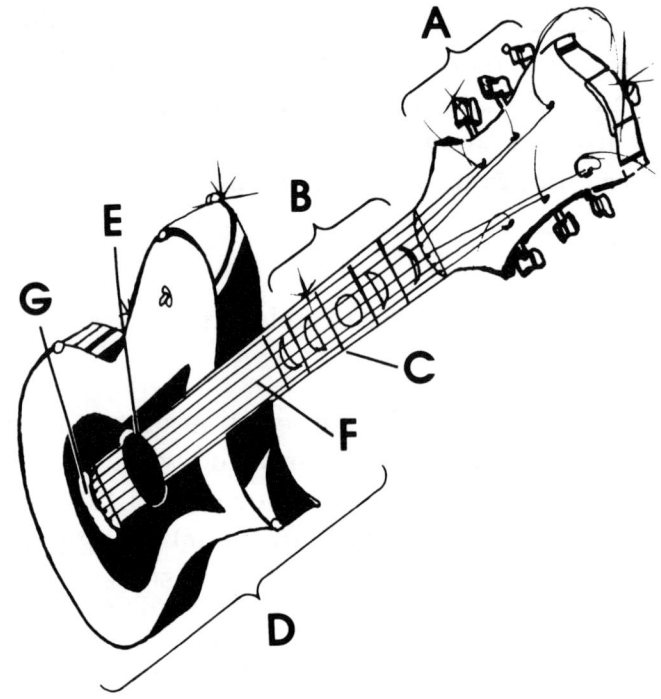

GUITAR PARTS

1. _____ body
2. _____ sound hole
3. _____ finger board
4. _____ frets

5. _____ strings
6. _____ bridge
7. _____ tuning pegs

The first sentence of the model introduces and describes the object that is defined in the paragraph.

8. What object is introduced? _____

9. How is it described? _____

Other sentences in the paragraph add to the definition by referring to specific characteristics of the subject. Next to each characteristic listed below, write those words from the model which help to define the guitar. Not all characteristics are referred to in the definition.

10. action _____

11. color _____

12. function _____

13. materials _____

14. parts _____

15. shape _____

16. size _____

17. texture _____

18. weight _____

19. The concluding sentence compares the guitar to other instruments. List them here.

   _____

Score the Practice exercise using the Answer Key, and go on to the Composition part of this guide.

Composition

This part of the guide will help you to apply what you have learned about writing a paragraph using definition. Choose **one** topic and list as many characteristics of the subject as you can find. Use this list as you follow the plan for writing a paragraph using definition.

You may find it helpful to use reference sources such as the dictionary, encyclopedia, or other books. When you use information from reference sources, do not copy directly from the book. Always use your own words to rephrase what you have read.

Topics

An airplane

A telephone

An umbrella

A shark

The human heart

Plan

- In the first sentence, introduce and describe the subject that will be defined in your paragraph.
- Write at least **five** sentences in which you define your subject as completely as possible. Use this list of characteristics as a reference: action, color, function, materials, parts, shape, size, texture, weight.
- Write a concluding sentence for your paragraph.

Use the Checklist to help you review and revise your writing. Do this for all drafts and your final copy.

Checklist   Yes   No

1. Before I began my paragraph, I listed characteristics of the subject.   ____ ____

2. In the first sentence, I introduced and described the subject that is defined in the paragraph.   ____ ____

3. I defined my subject in sentences which refer to specific characteristics. (Check [✓] those that apply):
   action ____ color ____ function ____
   materials ____ parts ____ shape ____
   size ____ texture ____ weight ____   ____ ____

4. I wrote at least five sentences of definition.   ____ ____

5. I wrote a conclusion for my paragraph.   ____ ____

6. I used my own words to rephrase what I read.   ____ ____

7. I used transitions to connect ideas and create unity in my writing.   ____ ____

8. I wrote complete sentences that begin with capital letters, and used proper end punctuation.   ____ ____

9. I proofread and edited my composition, and wrote a corrected copy of my work.   ____ ____

Submit the completed writing assignment and Practice exercise to your instructor for evaluation.

Comparison and Contrast

This guide will help you to write a paragraph using comparison and contrast. **We use comparison and contrast to explain how things are alike and how they are different.** The subjects you write about must have at least one category in common. You can compare dogs with cats because both belong to the same category, *household pets*. You can compare dogs with elephants because both belong to the same category, *animals*.

- When you **compare** one subject to another, you show how the two are alike, or similar. **The dog, like the cat, is a household pet**.

- When you **contrast** two subjects, you show how they are different. **The dog, unlike the cat, is very dependent on its master**.

- Sometimes, both **comparison and contrast** are used in the same sentence. **Both the dog and the cat make good household pets, but a dog requires more attention than a cat.**

Key Words

To write a comparison and contrast paragraph, you will need to use transitional words and phrases that express opposite points of view. You will also be using transitions that show relationships between ideas. We have grouped these key words in two categories below.

Key words commonly used to express **comparison** include:

like	similar	as
same	in the same way	too
both	most important	have in common
the same as	similarly	as well as

Key words commonly used to express **contrast** include:

although	yet	whereas
however	but	while
differ	instead	unless
unlike	on the contrary	contrary to
even though	on the other hand	the reverse

Practice

Read each part of the following exercise and answer all **28** questions. In the model paragraph below, the author explains two subjects by using comparison and contrast.

Apples and oranges are similar in some ways, yet they are also different. They are both fruits that grow on trees. Apples, however, do well in colder climates, while oranges grow best where it's hot year-round. The two fruits are both round and small, but their skins differ in thickness and in color. The orange is thick-skinned and orange in color, whereas the thin-skinned apple can be red, green, or yellow. You can eat the skin of an apple; however, the skin of an orange is inedible. The insides of both are juicy and delicious to eat. Most important, apples and oranges are very nutritious foods that satisfy your "sweet tooth."

Answer the questions below by filling in the blanks. Refer to the model to help you complete this exercise.

1. What two subjects are being compared in this paragraph?
   _____ and _____

2. To what general category do both of these subjects belong?
   _____

3. How many of the key words used in writing comparison and contrast can you find in the paragraph? _____

4. List **five** of the key words. _____

Listed below are characteristics of fruit that can be used in comparing and contrasting apples and oranges. Use the model to complete the chart below. Not every characteristic is referred to in the paragraph, so you will have some blanks. The first one is done for you.

84

CHARACTERISTIC	APPLES	ORANGES
where they grow	trees	trees
5. calories		
6. shape		
7. skin color(s)		
8. growing climate		
9. taste		
10. size		
11. skin (thick, thin)		
12. cost		
13. skin (edible, inedible)		
14. food value		
15. seeds		

For each of the following, indicate whether the sentence uses **comparison**, **contrast**, or **both**.

16. The banjo is very much like the guitar in its construction.
    _____

17. Day is light while dark is night.
    _____

18. Flowers and weeds are both plants, but people prefer flowers because of their beauty.
    _____

Comparison and Contrast

19. Lions, like tigers, are big cats that roam the jungle.
   _____

20. Although the dog is said to be man's best friend, cats are easier to care for.
   _____

21. Silver is less expensive than gold.
   _____

22. Although they have no arms, snakes can still climb as well as monkeys.
   _____

23. It's hot in the summer, but cold in the winter.
   _____

24. Both the sun and the moon are round.
   _____

25. The Civil War between the North and the South was, in some ways, similar to earlier wars.
   _____

26. Milk and soda are both beverages, but milk is a healthier drink.
   _____

27. Frank and John are the same height and weight, but John is much stronger.
   _____

28. Skiing, like ice skating, requires strong leg muscles and and a good sense of balance.
   _____

Score the Practice exercise using the Answer Key, and go on to the Composition part of this guide.

Composition

This part of the guide will help you apply what you have learned about writing a paragraph using comparison and contrast. Choose **one** topic and make a chart that compares and contrasts at least five characteristics of your subject. Use this list as you follow the plan for writing a paragraph using comparison and contrast.

Topics

Summer and winter

Youth and old age

Two sports of your choice

Men and women

Two of your friends

Plan

- Introduce the two subjects you will compare and contrast, and the category they have in common.

- Compare and contrast at least **five** characteristics of your subjects.

- Use the list of key words provided in the Practice exercise to help connect your ideas.

- Conclude your paragraph by telling the reader what you believe is the most important way in which your subjects are alike, or different.

Use the Checklist to help you review and revise your writing. Do this for all drafts and your final copy.

Checklist   Yes   No

1. Before I began my paragraph, I made a chart that compares and contrasts five characteristics of my subjects.   ____ ____

2. I began my paragraph by introducing the two subjects and the category they have in common.   ____ ____

3. I wrote sentences that compare and contrast at least five characteristics of my subjects.   ____ ____

4. I used key words associated with comparison and contrast to help connect ideas.   ____ ____
   These words are: _____

5. In my conclusion, I tell the reader the most important way in which my subjects are alike, or different.   ____ ____

6. I wrote complete sentences that begin with capital letters, and used proper end punctuation.   ____ ____

7. I proofread and edited my composition.   ____ ____

8. I wrote a corrected copy of my work.   ____ ____

Submit the completed writing assignment and Practice exercise to your instructor for evaluation.

Cause and Effect

This guide will help you to write a paragraph using cause and effect. Cause and effect are used to explain why something is the way it is. **The cause is the reason why, and the effect is the result.**

CAUSE
The boy stepped on a banana peel.

EFFECT
The boy fell.

The cause leads to the effect:

    The boy stepped on a banana peel and **he fell.**

        (cause) ⎯⎯⎯⎯⎯⎯⎯⎯→ (effect)

The effect is a result of the cause:

    The boy fell because **he stepped on a banana peel.**

        (effect) ←⎯⎯⎯⎯⎯⎯⎯⎯ (cause)

These are two different ways of saying the same thing about a cause and effect relationship.

Key Words

To write a cause and effect paragraph, you will need to use transitional words and phrases that help you restate main ideas. You will also be using transitions that show relationships between ideas. These key words are listed below.

if	thus	then	consequently
so	since	when	caused by
so that	because	due to	bring about
lead to	therefore	as a result	for this reason

Practice

Read each part of the following exercise and answer all **13** questions. In the model paragraph, the author uses cause and effect to explain how the custom of shaking hands came about.

> The custom of shaking hands developed as a result of fear and mistrust. At one time, men never went anywhere without a weapon because there was always the possibility of an attack. When strangers met, they made a point of moving their weapons aside and showing empty hands. Two men would join right hands in a firm clasp so that neither could reach for a dagger. If a man intended harm, he would never shake hands. Today, the clasping of hands is a way of introducing ourselves to others and saying that we are friend, not foe.

1. How many of the key words used to show cause and effect can you locate in the paragraph? _____

2. List the words. _____

Below are some statements based on the ideas presented in the model paragraph. Copy the sentences and write the word *cause* or *effect* in the parentheses that follow each phrase.

3. The custom of shaking hands (   ) developed because of fear and mistrust (   ).

4. Since most people carried weapons (   ), strangers signaled one another that they were friendly (   ).

5. Attack was always possible (   ); consequently, men brushed aside their weapons and showed empty hands (   ).

6. Men clasped their right hands (   ) so that neither could grasp a dagger (   ).

7. Suspicion (   ) led to the custom of shaking hands (   ).

The proverb below is a very old saying that uses cause and effect to tell the reader that even small details can be very important.

    For want of a nail the shoe was lost,
    For want of a shoe the horse was lost,
    For want of a horse the rider was lost,
    For want of a rider the battle was lost,
    For want of a battle the kingdom was lost,
    And all for the want of a horseshoe nail.

Copy the sentences below, and write the word *cause* or *effect* in the parentheses that follow each phrase. "For want of a nail" means the same thing as "because a nail was needed."

8. For want of a nail (   ) the shoe was lost (   ).

9. The horse was lost (   ) for want of a shoe (   ).

10. The rider was lost (   ) for want of a horse (   ).

11. For want of a rider (   ) the battle was lost (   ).

12. The kingdom was lost (   ) for want of a battle (   ).

13. All was lost (   ) for the want of a horseshoe nail (   ).

Score the Practice exercise using the Answer Key, and go on to the Composition part of this guide.

Composition

This part of the guide will help you apply what you have learned about writing a paragraph using cause and effect. Choose **one** topic and list five sets of causes and effects (how one thing leads to another). Use this list as you follow the plan for writing a paragraph using cause and effect.

You may find it helpful to use reference sources such as the dictionary, encyclopedia, or other books. When you use information from reference sources, do not copy directly from the book. Always use you own words to rephrase what you have read.

Topics

If I had three wishes

Laughter is good for you

Writing clearly is important

Major causes of the American Revolution

The law of gravity: what goes up must come down

Plan

- Introduce your subject in the first sentence of the paragraph.
- Write about your subject using cause and effect. Write at least **five** sentences for this part.
- Use the list of key words presented in the Practice exercise to help you connect ideas.
- Write a conclusion for your paragraph that summarizes the topic for the reader.

Use the Checklist to help you review and revise your writing. Do this for all drafts and your final copy.

Checklist	**Yes**	**No**
1. I listed sets of causes and effects about my topic. I began my paragraph by introducing the subject.	____	____
2. I wrote about my subject using cause and effect. I wrote at least five sentences for this part.	____	____
3. I used key words associated with cause and effect to help me connect ideas.	____	____
These words are: _____	____	____
4. I wrote a conclusion that summarizes my topic for the reader.	____	____
5. I used my own words to rephrase what I read.	____	____
6. I wrote complete sentences that begin with capital letters, and used proper end punctuation.	____	____
7. I proofread and edited my composition.	____	____
8. I wrote a corrected copy of my work.	____	____

Submit the completed writing assignment and Practice exercise to your instructor for evaluation.

The Persuasive Paragraph

This guide will help you to write a persuasive paragraph. **Persuasive writing appeals to your ability to reason and to your emotions.** This approach attempts to make the reader think, feel, and even act in a certain way. Persuasion is usually successful when the writer provides good reasons for doing, or not doing, something. Writing persuasively will convince the reader to see things **your** way.

Practice

Read each part of the following exercise and answer all **23** questions. In the model persuasive paragraph, the author attempts to convince the reader to stop smoking. He does this by relating his own experience with smoking and giving specific reasons why he quit.

> If you smoke cigarettes and want to stop, you can. I smoked for more than twenty years before I quit. I puffed in the face of danger, even though I was aware that smoking is linked to lung cancer, heart disease, and other potentially fatal diseases. Why worry about the future? The reason I did eventually quit was because I realized that the quality of my life was declining. I didn't enjoy eating because I couldn't taste my food. My social contacts, both personal and business, were negatively affected by the smoke I blew in other people's faces. Smoking also cut my energy level considerably. I had trouble exercising, playing sports, and even walking up stairs. Is this beginning to sound familiar? I finally quit smoking so that I could enjoy the rest of my life. You can do the same for yourself!

In the model, the author introduces the topic with a statement that challenges the reader to do something, in this case give up smoking. "If you smoke cigarettes and want to stop, you can." This strong opening sentence gets the reader's attention. The author then supports his argument throughout the paragraph by offering very specific reasons for giving up smoking and by stating his opinions.

1. The author reinforces his argument by pointing to the connection between cigarettes and disease. Write that sentence here:
   _____

2. The author further supports his argument with a firsthand account of how smoking affected his life. In how many ways was the quality of the author's life declining? _____

3. List each of the ways. _____

By addressing you directly, the author invites you to share his attitude toward the subject. Write the three sentences in which the author addresses the reader directly.

4. _____
5. _____
6. _____

In his conclusion, the author restates what he did, and why he did it. He then invites the reader to do the same. Write these two sentences.

7. _____
8. _____

Sentences based on ideas presented in the model are listed below. Some offer facts which appeal to reason. Other sentences offer opinions that appeal to the emotions of the reader. Write the word *fact* in the blank after each sentence that appeals to reason. Write the word *opinion* in the blank after each sentence that appeals to emotion.

9. I smoked for twenty years before I quit. _____

10. I wanted to enjoy my life. _____

The Persuasive Paragraph

11. Smoking is linked to lung cancer. _____

12. If you want to stop smoking, you can! _____

13. I puffed in the face of danger. _____

14. I had trouble exercising, playing sports, and climbing stairs.
    _____

15. Is this beginning to sound familiar to you? _____

16. Why worry about the future? _____

17. I couldn't taste my food. _____

18. People told me they didn't like smoke blown in their faces.
    _____

19. I didn't enjoy eating. _____

20. Smoking cut my energy level considerably. _____

21. I felt the quality of my life was declining. _____

22. I finally stopped smoking cigarettes. _____

23. You can do the same for yourself. _____

Score the Practice exercise using the Answer Key, and go on to the Composition part of this guide.

Composition

This part of the guide will help you apply what you have learned about writing a persuasive paragraph. Choose **one** topic and make a list of facts and another of opinions about the issue you have selected. You can argue for or against this issue. Use your lists as you follow the plan for writing a persuasive paragraph in which you try to convince the reader to accept your point of view.

Topics

Gossip is harmless.

We need to protect our environment from pollution.

Violence on television is harmful to children.

Every citizen should exercise his or her right to vote.

In this electronic age, reading and writing are not important.

Plan

- In your first sentence, make a strong statement or ask a question that gets the reader's attention.

- Write at least **five** sentences in which you offer facts and opinions that support your argument.

- Conclude the paragraph by suggesting an outcome for the reader to consider which further supports your argument.

Use the Checklist to help you review and revise your writing. Do this for all drafts and your final copy.

Checklist   Yes   No

1. I made one list of facts and another of
   opinions about my subject.   ____   ____

2. The first sentence of my paragraph is a
   strong statement, or question, that gets the
   reader's attention.   ____   ____

3. I wrote at least five sentences in which I offer
   facts and opinions that support my argument.   ____   ____

4. I concluded my paragraph by suggesting an
   outcome for the reader to consider which
   further supports my argument.   ____   ____

5. I used transitions to connect ideas and create
   unity in my writing.   ____   ____

6. I wrote complete sentences that begin with
   capital letters, and used proper end
   punctuation.   ____   ____

7. I proofread and edited my composition.   ____   ____

8. I wrote a corrected copy of my work.   ____   ____

Submit the completed writing assignment and Practice exercise to your instructor for evaluation.

The Essay

This guide will help you to write an essay. Any of the strategies you have used to write paragraphs can be applied in writing essays. Both the paragraph and the essay are similar in that each introduces a subject, offers supporting details, and draws conclusions. The difference is that an essay is more extensive and more fully developed.

- The first paragraph of an essay introduces the topic and may indicate a plan for its development.
- The middle paragraph or paragraphs develop the topic with supporting details: facts, descriptions, examples, and opinions.
- The concluding paragraph restates the topic and summarizes the main points of the essay.

Practice

Read each part of the following exercise and answer all **20** questions. In the model essay, the author uses narration to help explain (exposition) how the toothbrush and toothpaste were invented. This expository essay traces events in a chronological order and uses transitions to mark time.

Can you imagine cleaning your teeth without a toothbrush or toothpaste? That is exactly what people did until William Addis, an Englishman, invented the toothbrush. In 1770, Addis was arrested and sent to debtor's prison where he had ample time to use his lively and questioning mind. One morning Addis was cleaning his teeth in the usual way, with a rag, when an idea came to him. Wouldn't it be easier and more effective to *brush* teeth instead of wiping them?

The next day he picked out a small bone from a piece of meat he had for dinner and took it back to his cell. A guard supplied him with some stiff bristles. After boring holes into the bone, Addis tied the bristles together into tufts and wedged them into the holes, producing the first toothbrush. When Addis left prison, he went into business for himself. His toothbrush soon became a great success and the former debtor no longer had to worry about money.

For the next hundred years, people brushed their teeth by dipping toothbrushes into a porcelain jar of dental cream. A dentist from Connecticut decided that a more hygienic package for dental cream could be found. Dr. Washington Wentworth Sheffield had seen foods from other countries packaged in collapsible metal tubes. He figured that what worked for food could work for his new toothpaste as well. When *Dr. Sheffield's Cream Dentifrice* in a tube was introduced in 1892, it was an instant success.

Today, when we clean our teeth with a brush and toothpaste, we take the clean fresh taste this produces for granted. Now we know that credit for this pleasant experience belongs to Addis the prisoner and Sheffield the dentist for their practical inventions. While these two men had very different careers, they both saw a need and thought of a way to improve people's lives.

The Introductory Paragraph

Write the sentence that asks a question which appeals to the reader's interest?

1. _____

Write the phrase that introduces the topic of the essay.

2. _____

Why was William Addis arrested and sent to prison?

3. _____

What did people use to clean their teeth at this time?

4. _____

What idea did Addis have?

5. _____

Development Paragraph One

This paragraph presents the steps that Addis took to create a toothbrush.

What did he do first?

6. _____

What did a guard contribute?

7. _____

What did Addis do next?

8. _____

What was the result of Addis' efforts?

9. _____

What did Addis do when he left prison?

10. _____

Development Paragraph Two

This paragraph traces the development of toothpaste.

In addition to a toothbrush, what did people use to brush their teeth?

11. _____

How did people put cream on their toothbrushes?

12. _____

What did a dentist from Connecticut decide?

13. _____

What was the name of the dentist?

14. _____

How did he package dental cream?

15. _____

When did Dr. Sheffield introduce his *Cream Dentifrice*?

16. _____

The Concluding Paragraph

Write the sentence that reminds the reader of the topic of the essay.

17. _____

What details are repeated here to reinforce the main points of this essay?

18. _____

What opinion does the author express in concluding this essay?

19. _____

Time in this essay is marked through the use of dates and transitional words and phrases. List these in the order in which they appear.

20. _____

Score the Practice exercise using the Answer Key, and go on to the Composition part of this guide.

Composition

This part of the guide will help you apply what you have learned about writing an essay. Write your essay about **one** of the topics listed below. If you want to write about something else, consult with your instructor to determine if the topic is appropriate. Apply what you have learned from previous guides. You may find it helpful to use reference sources to gather facts about your topic. Follow the outline provided to write your composition. If you want more practice in writing essays, select other topics from the list below.

Topics

How a significant discovery was made (**expository**)

A decision that changed my life (**narrative**)

An exciting sports event (**descriptive**)

Why read the newspaper? (**persuasive**)

Travel: where I would go, what I would do (**expository**)

Outline

I. The Introductory Paragraph

   A. Begin with a strong statement, or question, that appeals to the reader's interest.

   B. Introduce the topic of your essay

   C. State or imply a plan for development:

   1. In an expository essay events are likely to be presented in chronological order.

   2. In a narrative essay introduce the setting, characters, and background information.

3. In a descriptive essay, use vivid details to introduce the setting and create a mood.

4. In a persuasive essay present your argument using both facts and opinions.

II. Development Paragraph(s)

A. Indicate what this paragraph is about.

B. Offer specific details that relate to your topic and are consistent with the strategy you are using:

1. In the expository essay, use each development paragraph to examine aspects of your subject. Present information in chronological order showing how one step leads to the next.

2. In the narrative essay, use each development paragraph to examine aspects of the plot. Tell what is happening, to whom, and why.

3. In the descriptive essay, use each development paragraph to appeal to one or more of the five senses. Create atmosphere by offering vivid details.

4. In the persuasive essay, use the development paragraphs to present each of your major arguments. Offer facts and opinions that convince the reader to see things your way.

C. Use transitions to link ideas within paragraphs and to make connections between paragraphs.

III. The Concluding Paragraph

A. Remind the reader of the topic of the essay.

B. Repeat important details to reinforce the main point.

C. Summarize or express your opinion to conclude the essay.

Use the Checklist to help you review and revise your writing. Do this for all drafts and your final copy.

Checklist   Yes   No

1. In my introductory paragraph I appeal to the reader's interest, state the topic of the essay, and state or imply a plan for the kind of essay I wrote.   ____   ____

2. In my development paragraph(s), I present details relevant to the topic and appropriate for the kind of essay I am writing.   ____   ____

3. In my concluding paragraph, I remind the reader of the topic, repeat important details, and summarize or express my opinion.   ____   ____

4. I use transitions to connect ideas and create unity in my writing.   ____   ____

5. I wrote complete sentences that begin with capital letters, and used proper end punctuation.   ____   ____

6. I proofread and edited my composition.   ____   ____

7. I wrote a corrected copy of my work.   ____   ____

Submit the completed writing assignment and Practice exercise to your instructor for evaluation.

List of Transitions

Transitional words and phrases can help you achieve coherence and unity in your writing. Use transitions to link ideas within paragraphs and to make connections between paragraphs. Connect your ideas with transitions in order to show time relationships, or place and position. You can also use transitions to express relationships between ideas, show comparison and contrast, or make summary statements and draw conclusions. You will find that some writing strategies make use of one kind of transition more than another. Transitions are grouped here according to the ways in which they function in writing.

TIME RELATIONSHIPS

after	first	second
after a while	following	secondly
after that	for a long time	several years ago
afterwards	forever	slowly
always	fourth	someday
as	from time to time	sometimes
as soon as	immediately	soon
at	in other times	sooner
at length	in retrospect	still
at the end	in some ages	subsequently
at the same time	in the end	suddenly
before	in the future	then
begin by	in the meantime	third
by the time	last	thirdly
constantly	later	this time
currently	long past	today
during	meanwhile	too often
endlessly	next	until
early	next time	usually
earlier	now	when
even now	now and again	whenever
even then	often	while
eventually	once	
finally	only when	

PLACE AND POSITION

above	everywhere	next
across	far	next to
adjacent	finally	on
adjacent to	first	one after another
ahead	former	opposite
along	from	out of
along the way	from aloft	outside
alongside	here	over
amid	horizontally	parallel
amidst	in	primarily
among	in front of	second
around	in the back	secondarily
at	in the background	there
at first	in the distance	third
at the end	in the first place	through
at the side	in the foreground	throughout
behind	in the front of	toward
below	in the midst of	under
beneath	inside	upon
beside	into	vertically
between	last	where
beyond	latter	within
by	near	
down	nearby	

RELATIONSHIPS BETWEEN IDEAS

about	as a consequence	begin by
about this	as a result	begin with
according to	as an illustration	besides
accordingly	as for	between
actually	as if	both
all this	as it stands	bring about
along with	as it worked out	but
also	as long as	by
although	as much as	certainly
almost	as though	contrary to
and	as well as	consequently
another	at least	despite
apparently	because	differ
as	because of	due to

RELATIONSHIPS BETWEEN IDEAS (continued)

either . . . or	instead of	rather than
equally	just	regardless of
especially	just as	same
even	lead to	seemingly
even as	like	similar
even if	likely	similarly
even then	likely to	simply
even though	likewise	since
except	mainly	so
except for	may be	so that
except that	maybe	specifically
finally	merely	such as
for	might well	surely
for example	more important	the fact that
for instance	more importantly	the reason for
for one thing	moreover	the reverse
for that reason	most important	the same as
for this reason	most importantly	then
from	most likely	there comes a time
from time to time	namely	there is every indication
further	naturally	that
furthermore	neither . . . nor	thereby
granted	nevertheless	therefore
have in common	no matter	though
however	no matter that	thus
if	no matter what	to be sure
if need be	not only	too
if only	not to mention	too often
important	obviously	unless
in addition	of	unlike
in addition to	of course	usually
in effect	on the basis of	what's more
in fact	on the contrary	whereas
in order to	on the other hand	when
in some cases	one of the reasons	whether
in spite of	only	whether or not
in the same way	only when	while
in this respect	or	with
in this situation	other than	with respect to
in turn	otherwise	yet
indeed	perhaps	
instead	probably	

COMPARISON

alike	in like manner	not only
as	in the same way	or
as well as	less than	same
both	like	similar
compared with	likewise	similarly
have in common	more than	the same as
in comparison	none can compare with	too

CONTRAST

against	however	on the other hand
although	in contrast	still
as opposed to	in contrast to	the reverse of
at the same time	in spite of	than
but	instead	though
contrary to	instead of	unless
conversely	much less	unlike
despite	neither	whereas
differ	nevertheless	while
even though	nonetheless	yet
except	nor	
except that	on the contrary	

SUMMARY STATEMENTS/DRAWING CONCLUSIONS

accordingly	evidently	on the basis of
all this and more	finally	perhaps
also	for of course	since
and if	for this reason	so
as a result	hence	so that
as a result of	if	summarily
as for	inevitably	taken all together
as long as	in conclusion	there is every indication that
because	in retrospect	there is every reason to conclude
because of	in the simplest terms	
bring about	in view of	
can only lead to	it is evident	thereby
caused by	it seems	therefore
consequently	it turned out that	thus
due to	led to	
due to this	not only . . . but also	

Answer Key

The Complete Sentence

1. subj: log   vb: floats
2. subj: food   vb: is
3. subj: marbles   vb: spilled
4. F   5. C   6. G   7. A   8. H   9. B   10. D   11. E
12. I can come to the party, (and) I'll bring a cake.
13. I will help you with your work later, (but) I want to rest now.
14. Do you want to eat at eleven, (or) would you rather eat at twelve?
15. When you leave the room, _please close the door quietly._
16. If I can borrow a car, _I am going to the beach._
17. When I swim, _I like to wear goggles._
18. While we're on vacation, _my brother and I plan to go sailing._
19. _Please close the door quietly_ when you leave the room.
20. _I am going to the beach_ if I can borrow a car.
21. _I like to wear goggles_ when I swim.
22. _My brother and I plan to go sailing_ while we're on vacation.

23. If your answer is a complete sentence, you are correct.
    Some sample answers are:
    - The students are washing cars.
    - I saw the students washing cars.
    - The students who are washing cars are in my class.
    - Are the students washing cars?
    - Look at those students washing cars!

24. If your answer is a complete sentence, you are correct.
    Some sample answers are:
    - The artist is painting the sunrise.
    - She saw the artist painting the sunrise.
    - The artist painting the sunrise is very talented.
    - Did you see the artist painting the sunrise?
    - What a beautiful sunrise the artist painted!

25. My car has a flat tire, and I may have to walk to work.

26. I would have changed the tire, but I didn't have the tools to do it.

27. Can you change the tire, or do you want to call the service station?

28. She waited by the side of the road; many cars passed by without stopping.

29. He saw a white cloth tied to the radio antenna; he knew she needed help.

30. The man was kind; he changed the tire.

Answering Questions

1. no
2. no
3. yes
4. yes
5. no
6. yes
7. yes
8. yes
9. yes
10. no
11. no
12. yes
13. yes
14. no
15. no
16. no
17. no
18. yes

Transitional Words and Phrases

There are one or more correct answers for each blank.

1. Afterwards
   Eventually
   First
   Later
   Next
2. after
   before
   once
3. after
   afterwards
   eventually
   in the meantime
   later
   meanwhile
   next
   soon
   then
4. After
   Afterwards
   Eventually
   Later
   Now
   Soon
   Then
5. First
   Now
6. After
   Afterwards
   Next
   Second
   Then
7. Afterwards
   Meanwhile
   Next
   Now
   Then
8. After
   Afterwards
   Later
   Next
   Now
   Then
9. if
   since
   because
10. Because
    Since
    While
11. because
    if
    since
12. Even though
    While
13. also
    nevertheless
14. and
15. because
    if
    since
16. As long as
    Since
    Due to the fact that
    In view of the fact that
17. As a result of
    Because of
    Due to
    In view of
18. Consequently
    For these reasons
    Hence
    In conclusion
    So
    Summarily
    Thus
19. as a result of
    because of
    due to
20. As a result
    Evidently
    For this reason
21. Consequently
    Evidently
    In conclusion
    It is evident
    Thus
22. although
    but
    though
    yet
23. Although
    Though
    While
24. but
    however
    yet
25. Unless
26. but
27. Conversely
    However
    In contrast
    On the contrary
    On the other hand
    Yet
28. unless

115

Answer Key

Combining Sentences

1. Sunday
2. afternoon
3. autumn
4. early
5. perfect
6. stroll
7. park
8. leaves
9. trees
10. covering
11. colors
12. couple
13. young
14. holding hands
15. sparkling
16. rays
17. sun
18. brilliant
19. painting
20. alive
21. people
22. colors

Expanding Sentences

2. young: adj
   women: subj (n)
   wearing: vb
   straw: adj
   hats: n
   flowered: adj
   shawls: n
   proudly: adv
   prepared: vb
   for the festivities: prep. phrase
   festivities: n

3. Every: adj
   October: n
   thousands: adj
   grey: adj
   whales: subj (n)
   leave: vb
   Chukchi Sea: n
   in search of warmer waters: prep. phrase
   warmer: adj
   waters: n

4. large: adj
   green: adj
   bullfrog: subj (n)
   croaked: vb
   loudly: adv
   splashed: vb

	into the water:	prep. phrase
	water:	n
5.	holiday:	adj
	crowd:	subj (n)
	waited:	vb
	restlessly:	adv
	for the fireworks to begin:	prep. phrase
	fireworks:	n
	begin:	vb
6.	along the creek:	prep. phrase
	creek:	n
	small:	adj
	grey:	adj
	black:	adj
	raccoon:	subj (n)
	drank:	vb
	cool:	adj
	water:	n
	daintily:	adv
	washed:	vb
	furry:	adj
	paws:	n
7.	stream:	subj (n)
	swirled:	vb
	lazily:	adv
	over mossy rocks and wooden logs:	prep. phrase
	mossy:	adj
	rocks:	n
	wooden:	adj
	logs:	n
	before it emptied into a lake:	prep. phrase
	emptied:	vb
	lake:	n
8.	young:	adj
	runner:	subj (n)
	raced:	vb
	aggressively:	adv

	to win first place:	prep. phrase
	win:	vb
	first	adj
	place	n
9.	We:	subj (pron)
	happily:	adv
	roasted:	vb
	marshmallows:	n
	over an open fire:	prep. phrase
	open:	adj
	fire:	n
10.	mountains:	subj (n)
	clothed:	vb
	in blue and purple:	prep. phrase
	blue:	adj
	purple:	adj
	because of the angle of the sun:	prep. phrase
	angle:	n
	sun:	n
	in the sky:	prep. phrase
	sky:	n
11.	She:	subj (pron)
	climbed:	vb
	up into the dark, dusty attic:	prep. phrase
	dark:	adj
	dusty:	adj
	attic:	n
	cautiously:	adv
	explored:	vb
	contents:	n
12.	In one closet:	prep. phrase
	one:	adj
	closet:	n
	of the old mansion:	prep. phrase
	hung:	vb
	threadbare:	adj
	wool:	adj
	coats:	subj (n)

with fur collars and velvet lapels:	prep. phrase
fur:	adj
collars:	n
velvet:	adj
lapels:	n

13.
woods:	subj (n)
already:	adv
filled:	vb
shadows:	n
bright:	adj
sunset:	n
still:	adv
glimmered:	vb
faintly:	adv
among the trunks of the trees:	prep. phrase
trunks:	n
trees:	n

14.
At the edge of the cliff:	prep. phrase
edge:	adj
cliff:	n
stood:	vb
lighthouse:	subj (n)
beacon:	n
constantly:	adv
circling:	vb
in the night:	prep. phrase
night:	n

15.
chocolate:	adj
pudding:	subj (n)
placed:	vb
on the table:	prep. phrase
table:	n
beside the luscious, freshly whipped cream:	prep. phrase
luscious:	adj
freshly:	adv
whipped:	vb
cream:	n

Paragraph Development

1. Anyone can build a campfire.

2. You begin with some wood shavings or small, dry twigs.

3. On top of that you place some larger twigs or thin branches.

4. When you begin to pile on the heavier wooden pieces, use a crisscross pattern.

5. This leaves plenty of space for the fire to come through.

6. Light the wood shavings or dried twigs with a match, and the job is done.

7. There is nothing complicated about building a campfire.

8. When I was little, my older sister was always trying to scare me.

9. She would jump out, screaming, from under the staircase.

10. She would turn the lights off and hold a flashlight under her chin.

11. She told frightening tales (stories).

12. Now, I laugh whenever I recall how easily my sister could scare me when I was young.

13. When I looked through our family photo album last Sunday, I was reminded of all the good times we had during our summer vacation.

14-16. Any three of the following are correct: fishing, taking pictures (photography), water skiing, boating, visiting amusement parks, riding the water flume.

17. Summer vacations are great because I always have a wonderful time.

The Narrative Paragraph

1. disobedient; ill-tempered

2. It is late afternoon.

3. "It was getting dark fast by then"

4. The story takes place in the woods.

5. "didn't seem to be anything alive around"
   "stumbled over a hidden rock"
   "scratched and sore all over"

6. The author is writing about a young person.

7. "He got up and almost cried . . ."
   ". . . he began to shoot the gun just to get used to it."

8. He's trying to get used to shooting a gun.

9. "he began to shoot the gun just to get used to it"

10. The character feels like crying. He is unhappy and scared.

11. "almost cried"
    "not very happy"
    "He was scared, too, and he said a prayer a minute . . ."

12. The character in this paragraph consoles himself by praying.

13. ". . . he said a prayer a minute and meant every word of what he said."

The Descriptive Paragraph

1. • towered thirty feet above half the trees
   • great evil god
2. none
3. none
4. none
5. none
6. • leg
   • piston
   • thousand pounds of white bone
   • thick ropes of muscle
7. none
8. none
9. a piston moving
10. thick ropes
11. • thigh
    • ton of meat
12. none
13. none
14. none
15. none
16. • two delicate arms dangled
    • hands pick up men like toys
17. none
18. none
19. none
20. hands that pick up men
21. snake neck coiled
22. none
23. none
24. none
25. none
26. • mouth hung open
    • teeth like daggers
27. none
28. none
29. none
30. teeth like daggers
31. eyes rolled
32. none
33. none
34. none
35. none
36. They (the eyes) showed hunger
37. hunger
38. none
39. none
40. none
41. • closed mouth
    • death grin
42. none
43. none
44. closed its mouth
45. none

The Expository Paragraph

1. E   2. I   3. A   4. D   5. F

6. B   7. G   8. H   9. C

10. The subject of this paragraph is how to prepare for spearfishing.

11. The author presents information in a sequence of preparatory steps.

12. fifteen   13. eleven

For questions 14-23, the following words in any order are correct:

14-23.
although	if	next
and	before	when
first of all	once	then
so/so that		

Using Examples

1. Few Americans will walk anywhere if they can help it, either for practical purpose or for pleasure.

Answers for 2-7 can be in any order.
2. banking
3. mailing letters
4. watching films
5. store shopping
6. restaurant service
7. "drive-in" church

8. cars: Corvette, Ford, Mercedes, Toyota

9. entertainment: concert, disco, movie, museum

10. feelings: angry, delighted, excited, scared

11. food: cheeseburger, pizza, salad, tacos

12. planets: Earth, Mars, Pluto, Saturn

13. relatives: aunt, brother, cousin, grandmother

14. seasons: fall, spring, summer, winter

15. sports: basketball, golf, soccer, tennis

16. other: lipstick, purple, sailboat, twelve

Using Definition

1. D 2. E 3. B 4. C

5. F 6. G 7. A 8. the guitar

9. a handheld, stringed, musical instrument made of wood

10. played by pressing strings against frets with one hand while strumming guitar with other

11. none   12. musical instrument

13. made of wood; strings of nylon or steel

14. body, sound hole, finger board, frets, strings, bridge, and tuning pegs

15. box, flat, hollow, pear or figure eight, circular opening

16. handheld; long piece of wood   17. none

18. hollow inside   19. banjo, mandolin, ukulele, violin

Comparison and Contrast

1. apples and oranges   2. fruits   3. seven

4. any five of the following: similar, both, however, while, but, differ, whereas, most important

APPLES	ORANGES
5. not applicable	not applicable
6. round	round
7. red, green, or yellow	orange
8. cold	hot
9. juicy and delicious	juicy and delicious
10. small	small
11. thin	thick
12. not applicable	not applicable
13. edible	inedible
14. nutritious	nutritious
15. not applicable	not applicable

16. comparison
17. contrast
18. both
19. comparison
20. contrast
21. contrast
22. both
23. contrast
24. comparison
25. comparison
26. both
27. both
28. comparison

125
Answer Key

Cause and Effect

1. five
2. as a result, because, when, so that, if
3. effect, cause
4. cause, effect
5. cause, effect
6. effect, cause
7. cause, effect
8. cause, effect
9. effect, cause
10. effect, cause
11. cause, effect
12. effect, cause
13. effect, cause

The Persuasive Paragraph

1. I puffed in the face of danger, even though I was aware that smoking is linked to lung cancer, heart disease, and other potentially fatal diseases.

2. six

3. He didn't enjoy eating.
   His social contacts didn't like smoke in their faces.
   Smoking cut his energy level.
   He had trouble exercising.
   He had trouble playing sports.
   He had trouble walking up stairs.

4. If you smoke cigarettes and want to stop, you can.

5. Is this beginning to sound familiar?

6. You can do the same for yourself!

7. I finally quit smoking so that I could enjoy the rest of my life.

8. You can do the same for yourself!

9. fact
10. opinion
11. fact
12. opinion
13. opinion
14. fact
15. opinion
16. opinion
17. fact
18. fact
19. opinion
20. fact
21. opinion
22. fact
23. opinion

The Essay

1. Can you imagine cleaning your teeth without a toothbrush or toothpaste?

2. ... William Addis, an Englishman, invented the toothbrush.

3. He was sent to debtor's prison because he owed people money.

4. a rag

5. It would be easier and more effective to brush teeth instead of wiping them.

6. He picked out a small bone from a piece of meat he had for dinner.

7. The guard supplied some stiff bristles.

8. He bored holes into the bone, tied the bristles together into tufts, and wedged them into the holes.

9. the first toothbrush

10. He went into business making and selling toothbrushes.

11. dental cream

12. by dipping into a porcelain jar filled with dental cream

13. that a more hygienic package for dental cream could be found

14. Dr. Washington Wentworth Sheffield

15. in collapsible metal tubes

16. 1892

17. Today, when we clean our teeth with a brush and toothpaste, we take the clean fresh taste this produces for granted.

18. ... credit for this pleasant experience belongs to Addis the prisoner and Sheffield the dentist for their practical inventions.

19. While these two men had very different careers, they both saw a need and thought of a way to improve people's lives.

20. | | | |
|---|---|---|
| until | after | for the next hundred years |
| in 1770 | when | today |
| one morning | soon | now |
| the next day | | |